The Poetry of Laurence Binyon

Volume VIII - England & Other Poems

Robert Laurence Binyon, CH, was born on August 10th, 1869 in Lancaster in Lancashire, England to Quaker parents, Frederick Binyon and Mary Dockray.

He studied at St Paul's School, London before enrolling at Trinity College, Oxford, to read classics.

Binyon's first published work was Persephone in 1890. As a poet, his output was not prodigious and, in the main, the volumes he did publish were slim. But his reputation was of the highest order. When the Poet Laureate, Alfred Austin, died in 1913, Binyon was considered alongside Thomas Hardy and Rudyard Kipling for the post which was given to Robert Bridges.

Binyon played a pivotal role in helping to establish the modernist School of poetry and introduced imagist poets such as Ezra Pound, Richard Aldington and H.D. (Hilda Doolittle) to East Asian visual art and literature. Most of his career was spent at The British Museum where he produced many books particularly centering on the art of the Far East.

Moved and shaken by the onset of the World War I and its military tactics of young men slaughtered to hold or gain a few yards of shell-shocked mud Binyon wrote his seminal poem *For the Fallen*. It became an instant classic, turning moments of great loss into a National and human tribute.

After the war, he returned to the British Museum and wrote numerous books on art; especially on William Blake, Persian and Japanese art.

In 1931, his two volume Collected Poems appeared and in 1933, he retired from the British Museum.

Between 1933 and 1943, Binyon published his acclaimed translation of Dante's *Divine Comedy* in an English version of terza rima.

During the Second World War Binyon wrote another poetic masterpiece *'The Burning of the Leaves'*, about the London Blitz.

Robert Laurence Binyon died in Dunedin Nursing Home, Bath Road, Reading, on March 10th, 1943 after undergoing an operation.

Index of Contents

ENGLAND

Shall we but turn from braggart pride
Our race to cheapen and defame?
Before the world to wail, to chide,
And weakness as with vaunting claim?
Ere the hour strikes, to abdicate
The steadfast spirit that made us great,
And rail with scolding tongues at fate?

If England's heritage indeed

Be lost, be traded quite away
For fatted sloth and fevered greed;
If, inly rotting, we decay;
Suffer we then what doom we must,
But silent, as befits the dust
Of them whose chastisement was just.

But rather, England, rally thou
Whatever breathes of faith that still
Within thee keeps the undying vow
And dedicates the constant will.
For such yet lives, if not among
The boasters, or the loud of tongue
Who cry that England's knell is rung.

The faint of heart, the small of brain,
In thee but their own image find:
Beyond such thoughts as these contain
A mightier Presence is enshrined.
Nor meaner than their birthright grown
Shall these thy latest sons be shown,
So thou but use them for thine own.

By those great spirits burning high
In our home's heaven, that shall be stars
To shine, when all is history
And rumour of old, idle wars;
By all those hearts which proudly bled
To make this rose of England red;
The living, the triumphant dead;

By all who suffered and stood fast
That Freedom might the weak uphold,
And in men's ways of wreck and waste
Justice her awful flower unfold;
By all who out of grief and wrong
In passion's art of noble song
Made Beauty to our speech belong;

By those adventurous ones who went
Forth overseas, and, self-exiled,
Sought from far isle and continent
Another England in the wild,
For whom no drums beat, yet they fought
Alone, in courage of a thought
Which an unbounded future wrought;

Yea, and yet more by those to-day

Who toil and serve for naught of gain,
That in thy purer glory they
May melt their ardour and their pain;
By these and by the faith of these,
The faith that glorifies and frees,
Thy lands call on thee, and thy seas.

If thou hast sinned, shall we forsake
Thee, or the less account us thine?
Thy sores, thy shames on us we take.
Flies not for us thy famed ensign?
Be ours to cleanse and to atone;
No man this burden bears alone;
England, our best shall be thine own.

Lift up thy cause into the light!
Put all the factious lips to shame!
Our loves, our faiths, our hopes unite
And strike into a single flame!
Whatever from without betide,
O purify the soul of pride
In us; thy slumbers cast aside;
And of thy sons be justified!

SIRMIONE

Give me thy hand, Belov'd! I cannot see;
So close above our steps, from tree to tree,
Shadows hang over us. How huge and still
Night sleeps! and yet a murmur, a low thrill,
Sighed out of mystery, steals slowly near,
Solitary as longing or as fear,
Through the faint foliage, stirring it, and shy
Amid the stillness, ere it tremble by,
Touches us on the cheek and on the brow
Light as a dew-dipt finger! Listen now,
'Tis not alone the hushings of the bough,
But on the slabbed rock-beaches far beneath
Listen, the liquid breath
Of the vast lake that rustles up all round
Whispering for ever! Soon shall we be where
The trees end, and the promontory bare
Breathes all that wide and water-wandering air
Which shall our foreheads and our lips delight,
Blown darkly through the breadth and depth and height
Of soft, immense, and solitary Night

— Where is the Day,
Bright as a dream, that on this same cliff-way
Fretted light shadows on old olive stems,
By whose gray, riven roots, like scarlet gems,
The little poppies burned? Where those clear hues
Of water, melted to diviner blues
In the deep distance of each radiant bay,
But close beneath us, past the narrowed edge
Of shadow from sheer crag and jutting ledge,
Shallowing upon the low reef into gold,
A ripple of keen light for ever rolled
Up to the frail reed sighing on the shore?
Where are those mountains far-enthroned and hoar
Above the glittering water's slumbrous heat,
With old blanched towns sprinkled about their feet,
Lifting majestic shoulders, that each side
Of that steep misty northern chasm divide,
Where, ambushed in the dim gulf ere they leap,
Wild spirits of the Wind and Thunder sleep?
'Tis flown, that many-coloured dream is flown,
And with the heart of Night we are alone.

This is the verge. The promontory ends.
Now the soft branches cover us no more.
Abrupt the path descends:
But we will sit here, high above the shore,
Here, where we know what wild flowered bushes cloak
Old ruined walls, and crumbling arches choke
With mounded earth, though buried from our eyes
In dark now, as beneath dark centuries
That marble-towered magnificence of Rome,
From whose hot dust the passionate poet fled
Hither, and laid his head
Where these same waters laughed him welcome home.

It is all dark; but how the air breathes free!
Beloved, lean to me!
Feel how the stillness like a bath desired
With happy pressure heals our senses tired;
And drink the keen sweet fragrance from the grass
And wafts from hidden flowers that come and pass, —
None here but we, and we have left behind
Noise of the rough world, in its cares confined,
All with the daylight drowned
In darkness on this height of utmost ground,
Where under us the sighing waters cease
And over us are only stars and peace.

O Love, Love, Love, look up! Let thy head lean
Back on my shoulder. Ah, I feel the keen
Indrawing of thy breath, and thy heart beat
Under my arm, and sighing through thee sweet
The wonder of the Night that widely broods
Over us with her glittering multitudes.
O in Night's garden has a fountain sprung
That over old earth showers for ever young
A fairy splendour of still-dropping spray?
Or in mad rapture has enamoured May
Through the warm dusk mounted like wine, and towered
And in far spaces infinitely flowered,
Breaking the deep heaven into milky bloom?
So beautiful in this most tender gloom
Ten thousand thousand stars through height on height
Burn over us, how breathless and how bright!
Some mild, some fevered, some august and large,
Royal and blazing like a hero's targe,
Some faint and secret, from abysses brought,
Lone as an incommunicable thought!
They throng, they reign, they droop, they bloom, they glow
Upon our gaze, and as we gaze they grow
In patience and in glory, till the mind
Is brimmed and to all other being blind;
They hang, they fall towards us, spears of fire
Piercing us through with joy and with desire.

Ah me, Beloved, comes an alien gust,
A sudden cold thought, blowing bitter dust
Upon this rapture. They are dead, all dead!
'Tis but the beauty of Medusa's head
Gleaming on us in icy masks, that stare
From everlasting winter blind and bare;
They have no answer for our hearts that yearn,
They have no joy in burning, only burn
Upon their senseless motion.

Ah, no, no
Canst thou not feel the warm truth overflow?
Light to light answers, even as heart to heart,
And by their shining we in them have part
Lo, the same light that in the tiniest spark
Makes momentary beauty from the dark,
The light that blesses warm earth, and inweaves
A million colours in young flowers and leaves,
That our sick thoughts and melancholy eyes
Confounds with magical simplicities,
Yea, that by dawn's beginning shall unfold

Wide glimmering waters, and to glory mould
Frore peaks, wild torrents in the vales between,
And golden mists on lawns of living green,
'Tis the same light that now above us showers
These star-drops, white and fair as falling flowers;
And silent rings a cry from star to sun,
Through all the worlds, light, life and love are one!

Hush thy heart now, Beloved, hush to sink
Thy thought down, deep as the still mind can think;
Then climb as high as boldest thought can climb!
Were these dark heavens the unfathomed gulfs of Time,
So might we see bright peopling spirits star
The memoriless ages, burning far,
Splendid or faint, tempestuous or serene,
All quick and fiery spirits that have been,
From whose immortal ecstasies and pains
Drops of red life run sanguine in our veins,
Who lived and loved, and prodigally spent
Their strength, their prayers, upon one pure intent,
In whom no deed was willed, no lonely thought
Attempered and to sword-blade keenness brought,
But it has helped us, even us, for whom
They shine in glory from the ages' gloom.
But oh, it is not only these I see:
Look up, behold unnumbered hosts to be!
What shall we do for them, whose hope endears
Futurity's dark wilderness of years?
Heroes, that shall adventure and attain
What broke our wills in passion and in pain;
Sages, to find all that we vainly seek,
Poets, to utter all we cannot speak!
And they at last shall into strong towers build
The stones we bled to gather, the unfulfilled
House of our dream; what was but fable sung,
Or indignation on a prophet's tongue,
Made form and hue of life's own tissue, wrought
Into the rich reality of thought.
And women, ah, what majesty of fate
Is theirs, for whom the little is made great,
The tender strong; far-off they also wait
The glory of their burden. Love, what deep
Of mystery unfolds! Let thy heart leap, —
Lo, at thy bosom all the world to come,
A child! It waits, it watches, it is dumb,
Yet hearkens and desires; the vision grows
Before us, and behind us overflows,
Mingling, as throng on throng of stars o'erhead,

One undivided host, the mighty dead
The mightier unborn! Time is rent away;
There is no morrow, no, nor yesterday,
Nor here, nor there, nor sleeping, nor awaking;
But, like full waters into ocean breaking,
Lost at this moment in our hearts' high beating
The boundless tides of either world are meeting;
And by the love-cry in my heart that rings,
And by the answer in thy heart that? sings,
We feel, at once exulting and afraid,
Near to the glowing of the Hand that made
And out of earth, with divine fire instinct,
Moulded us for each other's need, and linked
Our brief breath with the eternal will. That light
Shall kindle, in the dulling world's despite,
The inmost of our spirits, burning through
The shadow of all we suffer, dream, and do,
As surely as mine eyes, new facultied
In vision to the estranging day denied,
Still shall behold, when this fair night is fled,
All the stars shine round thy beloved head.

RUAN'S VOYAGE

I

The mist has fallen over the isles,
And Ruan turns his boat for home.
The wind is down; with an oar he steers
The narrow races, where at whiles
To left or right through fog he hears
The low roar and short hiss of foam,
As either rock-sharp shore he nears.
Full glad at heart he guides for home,
Full gladly looks ere night to reach
The little haven, twilit beach,
And pleasant smell of the green earth,
That he has left three days ago;
To warm both hands before the glow
Of peats upon the cottage-hearth,
Where his gray father will be mending
The old nets, and his mother, bending
Over the fire, at his step uplook
From the pot that smokes in the ingle-nook.

Is it a sea-mew's cry that calls

Loud through the mist and wailing falls?
Suddenly the white veil lifted,
And in smoking coils was drifted.
Ruan felt a cry ring through him.
There on a jutting rock alone
Stood a woman crying to him;
White her hair was heedless blown;
'Mid gleaming surf the rock rose bare;
Her withered arms were stretched in prayer.
"Fisherman, fisherman, help!" she cried.
Ruan turned his boat aside
Swiftly in the eddying tide.

"Fisherman, take me in thy boat
And to my own home carry me,
To the isle of Melilot
That lies upon the western sea."

"How earnest thou on this stormy strand,
A barren rock that men avoid?"

"Robbers came upon our land,
Burnt and pillaged and destroyed.
Half our women folk they reft,
And me upon this rock they left."

"Where is this isle of Melilot?
For of all the isles I know it not"

"Come hither and take me in with thee
And I will guide thee across the sea."

Heavily Ruan thought on his home
In Westerness across the foam;
But he turned his oar and glided near;
As it were his mother, he lifted her.

She sat in the stern, cloaked and dim,
And through the chill mist guided him.

It seemed that day had never an end,
It seemed that sea had never a shore,
Such weary hours he seemed to bend
Upon his never-resting oar,
And felt the cold salt on his lip,
And from his hair the vapour drip;
But still the blank fog brooded round
Over an ocean without sound.

At last along the glassy seas
Crept faint upon his face a breeze,
And like a shadow soft and light
Stole up a little wave that knocked
Upon the stern; the boat was rocked;
He looked, and O heart-stilling sight!
She who sat there was not the same!
Before his eyes the winter old
Fell from her; the full hair outrolled
In splendour soft as springing flame,
Breathing out a perfume sweet,
Over her shoulders to her feet.

Now like a bloom her face became,
Her arms and bosom rounded fair,
And even then was Ruan 'ware
Of blueness breaking the white air
And his own shadow trembling there;
And ere his tongue strove into speech
The keel was grating on a beach.

When mortals gaze on goddesses,
So high the hope of our dreaming is,
The wonder loses fear, the charm
Drinks up the wonder; Ruan leapt
Upon a shore in sunshine warm,
And forth with him the Lady stept;
And each to the other lightly talked,
As 'twere their wont so, hand in hand,
To wander through a lovely land.
By solitary slopes they walked.
The mist was scattered, but still before them
Was blown in fleecy tuft and trail;
And tremulous mid the melting cloud,
Upon the bushes low that bore them
Were crimson flowers that danced and bowed,
And green leaves fluttered their edges pale.

II

In a moment's space behold
The blue noon fell to evening gold.
Suddenly before them stood
A palace silent in a wood,

A dream of the eyes when music fills the ear

By night, and through the lulled brain ebbs and flows,
Might build and colour so unearthly clear
So fair and strange a house as rose
On Ruan's eyes; such gleaming walls,
Delicate towers and airy porticoes.
Pillars of clear jade, whose pale capitals
Like tiger's claws were ivory, smooth and bright,
Upheld a lintel fair like fretted snows.
The carved work by its shadow glowed distinct;
No crevice but was brimmed with brooding light:
Upon the roof a bird of Atlas blinked,
Sun-drowned in splendour from the gorgeous West,
And preened his plumes with languid crest;
Open, beneath, a shadowy doorway stood;
And fragrant smoke from fires of citron wood
Beckoned to happy senses, and the guest
Bade cross the threshold, enter, and be blest.

By now they paused within a spacious room,
Curtained about with glimmering tapestries,
That in the hush and richness of the gloom
Hung like a forest gemmed with fancied eyes.
Pale tendrils twined about the clustered pipe
Of reeds, and black trunks branched above remote
To heavy fruit that hovered over-ripe
Of fiery gold and dull vermilion stripe,
A waste of boughs for wild birds' pillaging:
And over dimness large leaves seemed to float,
That here were spotted like an adder's throat
And there were greener than a finch's wing.
It seemed to live, though all was whist,
And Ruan gazing seemed to hear
With heart-throb quickened into fear
The drooping briars writhe and twist,
The branches wave with stealthy stir
Of dappled leaves or dappled fur —
A sound as if the tangle hissed!
He trembled as the room he scanned.
The Lady clasped him by the hand.
He looked into her face; she stole
In that moment all his soul
"Fear not, fear not, all is thine,
Ruan, so thou wilt be mine!
I am Morgaine, whom mortals call Le Fay,
And I have brought thee to my house this day
Because I love thee and will give thee more
Than thou hast dreamed in all thy life before."
With that she kissed him on the mouth, and he

Was like warm wax before her witchery;
And as she spoke the arras changed to view
Tender and tremulous and clear in hue
As April woods of white anemone;
And in his heart fear died to joy anew.

She led him on with willing feet.
Through many a perfumed hall they glided;
His brain grew giddy with that incense sweet,
But still the smile of Morgaine guided
Betwixt slim pillars, on a floor
Of brindled coromandel wood,
Where now 'twas scented dusk no more
But airy peace calmed all his blood,
For in the wall a window wide
Looked out on magic eventide.
Far, far beneath them a blue lake was cupped
Hollow amid the twilight of a vale,
And over wan mist floating frail
A rosy mountain soared abrupt.
Black pines and gold-green mosses there
On rocks whose distance none could tell
Were pictured in the soundless air
And rivulets that faintly fell
As in some gorge of Saianfu,
Where from her porcelain palace-tower,
Lone on a crag's mist-cradled throne,
A princess leans amid the dew
Of such a marvellous evening hour
O'er balustrade and precipice,
Her lute and woven silk laid by,
Dreaming with a sudden sigh
Of the world-enchanting kiss.

With such a sigh was Ruan's bosom heaving,
With such a sting of beauty past believing,
When soft beside him spoke Morgaine, "Come, tell:
O Ruan, doth my kingdom please thee well?"
"Princess, princess," he answered, "I am blest
Beyond all mortals: tell me thy behest
And I will be thy servant" But that word
She smiled away; his arms leapt round her, pressed
With mad joy, as she whispered "Be my lord!"

III

Morgaine, that lurest the souls of men that are greedy of joy,

What soughtest thou out, Morgaine, in the face of a fisher-boy?
Were the souls of the great ones of earth so easy a prey to thy snare,
Lightly bound to thy hand by a single shining hair,
That the simple heart of a youth, untempted, in hard ways bred,
To thy siren hunger is sweeter than kings or captains dread?
Thou sang'st him songs that lapped him in utter forgetfulness
Of the green hills and the rocks and the waters of Westerness,
Till Time, like a wandering light that is stayed on an opal, shone
Kindled and many-coloured; the charmed days moved not on.
His thoughts were borne as idly as clouds on the slow South,
Or a willow leaf that glides on a wandering summer stream,
And the light that bathed his body, and breathed so sweet to his mouth
Was such as mortals know but in splendid rents of dream
Piercing the cloud of sleep from the dull day-world beguiled.
Together they sailed the calm of evening waters isled
With knolls of gemmy grass, and thickets of nightingales;
They gathered flowers, and listened, and moved with drooping sails;
And anon they rose from a feast, from close-embowered delights,
To hunt the timid gazelles on passionate moonlit nights,
Blue nights of milky stars, where fluttering petals snowed
From windswept boughs and scented delicious dusk, and rode
Home by shadowy glades upon soft invisible lawn
Hand in hand through the dews of a shy dove-coloured dawn.
They drank of a fairy wine, till their hearts were weary of earth,
And them, embraced, the mighty wings of Phoenix bore
Up through the light exulting to soar and still to soar,
And the world dropped down beneath them; they clapped their hands in mirth
Mocking the baffled eagle: but how should mortal tell
What wonders Morgaine wove for Ruan in her spell
To charm the nights and days with hopes thatnever tire,
Morgaine of blissful body and eyes of far desire?

IV

Count the hours that bind and freeze,
That break the breast and shake the knees!
What need of Time's all-patient dial
To him that drinks of this deep phial?
These perfumed hours of white and red
Flowered and were never shed.
It might have been a morning's span
Or twice and thrice the years of man,
For Ruan was not Then nor Now;
He was as young as his desire, as young
As on sweet lips an old song newly sung.
O idle thought to number how
The days onrushed, the morrows flushed,

Thicker than blossoms on an apple-bough.

But on a morn at early dawn awaking
He saw the cold light through the lattice breaking.
A spider there her web had made;
Softly in the air it swayed.
Memory in a drowsy muse
Lost and sought such filmy clues.
Till upon a sudden plain
In Ruan's vision, sharp like pain,
Pictured was his home again,
And the long nets, loosely hung
From the white wall, stirred and swung.
He rose and broke into a mournful cry,
Which Morgaine heard with half-shut eye
And caught him with both hands and strove
To turn him with soft words of love,
But he would not; so sharp a pang
Of desolation in him sprang
For all the dearness long forgot
In his own kind's deserted lot;
A tear fell from his eyelids hot
Upon the marble floor below.
He wept; and in an instant, lo!
Beheld the floor transparent glow.
Yawning, a spectral region shone
Where cold abysses plunged betwixt
Sheer mountain column-peaks whereon
That very palace floor was fixt.
Ruan shuddered as he gazed.
For toward his eyes were eyes upraised
From human faces, forms that froze
Within the rock-walls as they rose,
A thousand forms, a prisoned host
Imbedded in the mountain frost

But swift a storm of wind and fire
Up those abysses roared and rushed;
The shapes were stirred; a vain desire —
As they would struggle, nearer, higher, —
Their eyes awoke, their bodies flushed.
And then the blast as sudden passed,
The limbs of torment slowly sank
To ice-green languor, fleshless bone,
And starving ruggedness of stone;
The life within them swooned and shrank
To dungeoned attitudes again,
Their half-closed upturned eyes alone

Were gazing in the gaze of pain.

With eyes of horror opened wide
"Save me, save me!" Ruan cried.
But Morgaine in her arms hath wound him,
Her panting fierce embrace hath bound him,
Her eyes exulting change and glow
Like lights upon a shaken sword.
She pants as in unearthly throe,
Her arms cling tighter than a cord;
How shall Ruan dare to brook
The demon challenge of her look?

"Listen, Ruan, canst thou hear
How the whole world cries in fear?
Lights not splendour in the air
To dance above the world's despair?
They toil in hunger, grief and night
For our desire, for our delight —
They the twisting roots, and we
The topmost red flower on the tree!"

But Ruan with both hands that pressed
Against the burning of her breast,
Trembled and groaned in that embrace,
And strove from that exultant face.
When soft she melted, sank before him, kneeled
And clung, beseeching him that would not yield.
"They are my flesh, my blood, and I
Must go to seek them, or I die."
When Morgaine heard that lamentable cry
She knew the heart of joy in him was dead,
Looked in his soul and saw her hour had fled.

"Go then," she wept, "but come again
To thy delight, to thy Morgaine.
Yet if thou go, this casket take with thee;
Hid in thy breast, 'twill guide thee safe to me
Without a rudder o'er the wandering sea.
But O beware thou never open this,
Else art thou lost and all thy hope of bliss.
Farewell!" she kissed him. "Farewell," Ruan said,
And took the casket with averted head,
Nor turned him back, but swiftly passed the door
Of the charmed house, and came to the sea-shore.

V

O what a calm as of old days come back
With their old wont and clear untroubled way
Lifted the heart of Ruan, on the track
Of ocean steering for his native bay!
Over blue waves the morning air sang sweet
Full on his sail; he was all fire to greet
The hearth of home, his father's joyful face,
His mother's tears and tremulous embrace.
He sailed beneath the summer's early noon
With the warm favouring wind; and strangely soon
Rose up the coast, till nearing on the swell
He saw the dark waves glitter as they fell
Against the cliff's worn bases, drained of foam.
Now he is past the headland. There is home!
The boats drawn up, the sands, and the green mound
Beyond them; peaceful, sunned, familiar ground,
It seemed he had not been three days away.
With a light heart he beached amid the spray
His boat, and moored it as of old, and sprang
Ashore; a young girl to a baby sang,
Sitting on fishing-nets spread forth to dry.
She looked up, and her song stopped, and her eye
Was filled with wonder; but impatiently
Ruan ran up the beach, where he might catch
The first glimpse of his father's cottage thatch.
He came, he looked; and the heart in him failed.
The house was not. What lonely strangeness ailed
The world? He thrust his hand within his vest
And felt the casket cold upon his breast.
Helpless he gazed: but lo, there slowly came
An old man with a stick, coughing and lame,
Bowed by his years; then towards him Ruan ran,
With a swift thought of pity, almost scorn,
In his young strength for such old age forlorn,
And cried upon the way, " Old man, old man,
Where is my father? Surely thou know'st me;
I am Ruan, Ruan! I am home from sea."
The old man lifted up his faint blue eye
And peered upon him slow and curiously
As on some strange thing from the sea upcast
"Nay, Ruan's name I know not," came at last
The answer. Ruan cried, "Dwell'st thou not here?"
"Ay, all my life, three-score and fifteen year."
"And yet thou know'st not Ruan? "The old man
Puzzled his withered brow as he began
Seeking some far-sunk memory in his brain.
"Ay, so it is;" he slowly spoke again,

"They told a tale of Ruan; ay, 'tis so.
How he was lost, but that was long ago,
Hundreds of years, I think; he sailed away,
And his old parents died of grief, they say."
He still spoke on; but Ruan heard no more,
For he was wandering fast along the shore
In the lone sunshine; aimlessly he strayed,
Dazzled and indescribably afraid.
On a sudden flamed a thought
Through his body: straight he sought
Within his breast the casket hid,
Crying, "Morgaine, thou shalt tell,
Though the answer come from Hell!"
With trembling fingers he undid
The silken cord, the golden lid.
Lo, from the opened casket broke
A stealing skein of purple smoke,
A wandering faint cloud of perfume
That rippled up in filmy plume,
And lingered faltering like a prayer,
Then melted into sunlit air.
Three hundred years had melted there,
Three hundred years of faery bliss,
Perished sooner than a single kiss!
As Ruan stares upon the empty box,
His outstretched fingers stiffen stark,
His cheek is shrivelled, his eyes grow dark,
Either knee together knocks;
Ere he can pray, ere he can groan,
Swift as grass in a furnace thrown,
Or a crumbled clod in a heedless hand,
He withers into whitened bone.
Where his breathing body stood,
Flushed with life and warm with blood
Is a heap of ashes, a drift of sand,
And the wind blowing, and the silent strand.

LOVE'S PORTRAIT

Out of the day-glare, out of all uproar,
Hurrying in ways disquieted, bring me
To silence, and earth's ancient peace restore,
That with profounder vision I may see.
In dew -baptizing dimness let me lose
Tired thoughts; dispeople the world-haunted mind,
With burning of interior fire refined;

Cleanse all my sense: then, Love, mine eyes unclose.

Let it be dawn, and such low light increase,
As when from darkness pure the hills emerge;
And solemn foliage trembles through its peace
As with an ecstasy; and round the verge
Of solitary coppices cold flowers
Freshen upon their clustered stalks; and where
Wafts of wild odour sweeten the blue air,
Drenched mosses dimly sparkle on old towers.

So, for my spirit, let the light be slow
And tender as among those dawning trees,
That on this vision of my heart may grow
The beloved form by delicate degrees,
The desired form that Earth was waiting for,
Her last completion and felicity,
Who through the dewy hush comes, and for me
Sings a new meaning into all Time's lore.

Just-dinted temples, cheek and brow and hair —
Ah, never curve that wind breathed over snow
Could match what the divine hand moulded there,
Or in her lips, where life's own colours glow,
Or in the throat, the sweet well of her speech;
Yet all forgotten, when those eyelids raise
The beam of eyes that hold me in their gaze
Clear with a tenderness no words can reach.

Some silken shred, whose fair embroidery throbbed
Once on a queen's young breast; a mirror dimmed
That has held how much beauty, and all robbed!
One bright tress from a head that poets hymned;
A rent flag that warm blood was spent for: sighs,
Faith, love, have made these fragrant, and sweet pain
Quickens its pangs upon our pulse again,
Charmed at a touch out of old histories.

But thou, whence com'st thou, bringing in thy face
More than all these are charged with? Not faint myrrh
Of embalmed bliss, dead passion's written -trace,
Half-faded; but triumphant and astir
Life tinges the cheek's change and the lips' red.
Thy deep compassions, thy long hopes and fears,
Thy joys, thine indignations, and thy tears,
To enrich these, what stormy hearts have bled!

For thine unknown sake, how has life's dear breath

Been cherished past despair: how, lifted fierce
In exultation, has love smiled at death,
For one hope hazarding the universe!
What wisdom has been spelled from sorrow's book,
What anguish in the patient will immured,
What bliss made perfect, what delight abjured,
That in these eyes thine eyes at last might look!

O mystery! out of ravin, strife, and wrong,
Thou comest, Time's last sweetness in the flower,
Life's hope and want, my never-ended song!
Futurity is folded in this hour
With all fruition; joy, and loss, and smart;
And death, and birth; the wooed, the feared, the unknown;
And there our lives, mid earth's vast undertone,
Are beatings of one deep and mighty heart.

FOREST SILENCE

Where she reclines
In a rock's cup,
Smooth, tawny-mossed,
Under tall pines,
Her eyes look up,
Her gaze is lost

Pine-plumes, sea-gray,
When air sings through
The rust-red stems,
Wave slowly, fray
The liquid blue
To flashing gems.

A lizard's haste
Rustles dead leaves;
A light cone drops;
Else this sweet waste
No sound receives
But stirred tree-tops.

A thrill of air
From far slow draws
Its long caress,
Sighed out no-where;
Then noon at pause
Drinks silentness.

But she; what waft
Of perfume brought
Her musing stirs?
What pure keen draught
Of wine-like thought
Even now is hers?

Her eyes dream dreams;
Coiled foot stirs not,
Nor idle hand.
Spell-drowsed she seems,
Hushed in some plot
Of faery land.

Yet soft, with such
Light lingerings felt
As when boughs part
Again to touch,
Spring, meet and melt
Within her heart

Hope, wish, and prayer,
And memory warm
From far hours, all
Newly aware
Of sudden charm
And wistful call

Out of lost years
Earth's mystery,
Strange with its pain,
Holy with fears,
Touches her, shy
As breeze, as rain.

And this rich hour
With feeling fills
Too full to hold
Its wealth — a flower
That trembling spills
Seed-spice of gold.

CHATEAU GAILLARD

Shattered tower and desolated keep

Darken; far below the river shines
Under cliffs that round the twilight sweep.
Rock-rough headlands on the sky's confines
Couch asleep.

Silence breathes; the air colours; dewy smell
Freshens keener from the grass; a hush
Deepens on some distant evening bell.
Burning out of heaven the solemn flush
Spins a spell;

Sharpens every shadowy edge of stone;
Notches gaps abrupt; drains pale the light;
Blackens gulfs of fosse, where mounds enthrone
What were towers. The ruin to soft night
Looms alone.

Lo, it lives! Now like a terrible thought
Seems it A man's strength, how frail beside
Yonder strength! Could hands of flesh have wrought
Such a thing? Mere ashes they that cried,
They that fought,

Where the little poppy spots with red
Crumbling bastions; dust of centuries, all
Those strong feet that over heaps of dead
Leapt, and hands that furious clutched the wall,
Breasts that bled.

Yet a presence, yet a power is here,
In the darkening silence slowly felt,
Silence that is naked and is near.
Into cloud those battle-rages melt;
But a fear

Strikes from where these pressing stones conspire
Toward a purpose past the strength of each,
As a man's deeds knit by one desire,
As a great verse out of casual speech
Forged in fire.

Stones no longer, having filled their place!
Nay, though tumbled, torn and cast aside,
Touched with glory Time cannot deface:
In such wreck, Man, scarred and glorified,
Builds his race.

Lion- Heart, thou buildedst not in vain,

Lion- Heart, that in our own blood still
Beatest; rent but royal over Seine
This the embattled proud child of thy will
Shall remain!

"O LOVE OF MY LIFE"

O Love of my Love, O blue,
Blue sky that over me bends!
The height and the light are you,
And I the lark that ascends,
Trembling ascends and soars,
A heart that pants, a throat
That throbs, a song that pours
The heart out as it sings.
Lo, the dumb world falls remote,
But higher, higher, the golden height!
Oh, I faint upon my wings!
Lift me, Love, beyond their flight,
Lift me, lose me in the light.

THE CLUE

Life from sunned peak, witched wood, and flowery dell
A hundred ways the eager spirit wooes,
To roam, to dream, to conquer, to rebel;
Yet in its ear a voice cries ever, Choose!

So many ways, yet only one shall find:
So many joys, yet only one shall bless;
So many creeds, yet to each pilgrim mind
One road to the divine forgetfulness.

I Tongues talk of truth; but truth is only found
Where the heart runs to be poured utterly,
Like streams whose home is in their motion, bound
To follow one faith and in that be free.

O Love, since I have found one truth so true,
Let me lose all, to lose my loss in you.

VIOLETS

Violets, in what pleasant earth you grew
I know not, nor what heavenly moisture stole
To tincture in your petals such dim blue
As seems a pure June midnight's scented soul:

But on her bosom when you breathed so sweet,
You were as lovely words to thoughts that rose
So deep in us, no language could complete
Their sense, nor half their tenderness unclose.

O in such thoughts Love ever freshly flowers.
They neither ask nor answer, only give
Their charm up to the kind and unkind hours,
Born of that beauty in whose light we live,

Whose grace is past all probing of our wit
And sweetens even the hand that bruises it

MOTHER AND CHILD

By old blanched fibres of gaunt ivy bound,
The hollow crag towers under noon's blue height
Ribbed ledges, lizard-haunted crannies white,
Cushioned with stone-crop and with moss embrowned,
Cool that clear shadow from the outer glare
Above a grassy mound,
Where she that sits, muses with lips apart
And eyes dream-filled beneath the abundant hair
And lets the thoughts flower idly from her heart

Thoughts of a mother! For her child amid
Lights blossoms that a brook's cold ripple fledge,
Wind-shaken at the shadow's glowing edge,
Plays with a child's intentness; now half-hid,
And now those gay curls caught in frolic sun
Toss to the breeze unbid
And through the thoughts of her who watches shine
With quiverings of felicity that run
Through all her being, as through water wine.

Her thoughts flow out to the stream's endless tune.
Ah, what full sea could all that hope contain?
Then apprehensions vivid like a pain
Wing after, swift as through this airy noon
The swallow skims and flashes past recall

But O returns how soon,
Back in a heart's beat! So her fears have sped
Far as the last loss — homing out of all
The deep horizon to that golden head.

The Child, amid the blossom, nothing recks.
His eyes a flame-winged dragon-fly pursue
Over stirred heads of mint and borage blue
In warm and humming air; on slender necks
Marsh-flowers peep toward him over juicy rush,
And the wild parsley flecks
With powdery pale bloom stalks his bare feet bruise,
And hot herb-odours mingle where they crush
Deep in the green growth and the matted ooze.

How smoothly clear along his ankle slips
The water, gliding to the pebbled cool!
He laughs with those young ripples of the pool.
Then the wind lifts a long spray's leafy tips
And dashes him with drops of twinkling fire
As in the stream it dips,
Where over shadows bright with wavering mesh
Bramble and thorn and apple-scented brier
Their roots and low leaves thirstily refresh.

His mother calls. Now over thymy sod
The boy comes, yet he lingers; the flowers keep
His feet among them, clustering fair and deep.
Red crane's-bill shakes its seed; milk-campions nod,
By the rough sorrel little pansies hide;
Slim spikes of golden-rod
Above the honeyed purple clover flame;
And, where the sheltered dew has scarcely dried,
Cling worts, close-leaved, each with its own wild name.

What secret purpose infinitely wrought,
Each in its lovely kind and character,
These breathing creatures in the light astir,
Articulating new an endless thought
That still with some last difference must refine
The likeness it had sought?
Some bloom to mateless glory will unfold,
A grace undreamed some airy tendril twine,
Some leaf be veined with unimagined gold.

Thee too, Child, with life budding in thy face
And quickening thy sweet senses, O thee too,
For whom the old earth maketh herself all new,

Each hour compels with unreturning pace
From the vague twilight being that keeps thee kin
To all the unconscious race,
Compels thee onward; for thy spirit apart
The habitation is prepared within;
The separate mind, the solitary heart

Is it a prison the slow days shall build,
When, disentwining from the world around,
Thou shalt at last gaze out of eyes unbound
On alien earth, with other purpose filled, —
Thou with the burden of identity,
Thou separately willed,
And feel at last the difference thine own
Mid thy companions, saying " This is I,
I, and none other in the world's mind alone."

Even now thine eyes are lifted from the flowers,
And the sky fills them : boundless and all pure,
Regions afar to thrilling silence lure.
Ah, how to charm the fret of future hours
Shall to thy mind come, as from wells of light
And time-forgetting powers,
Words large and blue and liquid as the sky;
The absolution of the infinite,
And sea-like murmur of eternity!

Shalt thou not long then, when the dark hours wring
Thy heart with pangs of mortal loss and doom,
That old unsevered being to resume
With its kind ignorance, relinquishing
This self that is so exquisitely made
For sorrow; time's dull sting
To lose, and the sharp anguish, and the wrong;
Into life's universal glow to fade,
And all thy weakness in that whole make strong?

Yet O thou heart so surely doomed to bleed,
Thou out of boundless and unshaped desire
Compacted essence single and entire,
Rejoice! In thee Earth doth herself exceed.
O tarrier among flowers, of thee the unplumbed
Infinities have need;
Or how shall all that dumbness speak, and how
Those wandering blind energies be summed
As in a star? Rejoice that thou art thou!

Mighty the powers that desolate and kill,

Armies of waste and winter: and alone
Thou comest against them in the might of one
World-challenging and world-accusing will.
Yet mightier thou that canst thy might refrain,
The world's want to fulfil,
Thy soul disprison from time's mortal hour,
To pardon and pity changing that old pain,
And in thy heart the eternal Love let flower.

All faith inhabits in thy Mother's eyes.
Yet she already hath all thy pangs foreknown
And in thy separation felt her own.
Far from her feet follow thy destinies!
There is no step she hath not trod before.
Her loss she glorifies
To spend on thee her all; and to defend
The divine hope which in her womb she bore,
Those arms of love wide as the earth extend.

LITTLE HANDS

Soft little hands that stray and clutch,
Like fern-fronds curl and uncurl bold,
While baby faces lie in such
Close sleep as flowers at night that fold,
What is it you would clasp and hold,
Wandering outstretched with wilful touch?
O fingers small of shell-tipped rose,
How should you know you hold so much?
Two full hearts beating you enclose,
Hopes, fears, prayers, longings, joys and woes —
All yours to hold, O little hands!
More, more than wisdom understands
And love, love only knows.

LULLABY

Sleep, sleep on Mother's breast,
Child, my child!
Close within my arms be pressed.
O the world is vast and wild,
Filled with hurt and war and cries!
Under my eyes close your eyes,
On my breast rest and nest.

Sleep come soft as water flows,
Eyes close bind!
Gentle Sleep that never grows
Old, indifferent, or unkind.
O but Sleep can never hold you
As my arms, my darling, fold you,
Fold you close, fold you close.

Sleep can take you far away,
Little heart!
O but in my heart you stay,
From my heart you cannot part,
Though the world you wandered, Sweet,
From my heart those little feet
Never stray, night or day.

"A DAY THAT IS BOUNDLESS AS YOUTH"

A day that is boundless as youth
And gay with delight to be born,
Where the waves flash and glide over sands
In their pure image rippled and worn;
Where laughter is young on the air
As the race of young feet patters light:
Linked shadows run dancing before
In the midst of the infinite light:
On a violet horizon asleep
One milky sail glimmers afar;
And our spirits are free of the world
With nothing to bind or to bar;
With no thought but the thoughts of a child; —
O golden the day and the hour!
The strong sea is charmed from his rage,
And the waste is more fair than a flower.

A WINTER SONG

Now December darkens
Over Autumn dead.
The frozen earth now hearkens
For the last leaf to be shed.
Above gray grass the branches bare
Melt, faint ghosts, in misty air,

Like despair.

O the nearer, deeper
In my heart, remembering
My Love's kiss, and how her eyes
Blessed me like enchanted skies,
Is the joy that with the spring
Shall waken Earth the sleeper.

A SPRING SONG

Not yet a bough to bud may dare
On the naked tree.
Yet happy leaves in the bough prepare;
And could I see
Far as a soaring bird, I know
Where young in sheen
The willow, swaying soft and slow,
Laughs gold and green.

O in our winter's heart to build
A tower of song!
My Love should enter when she willed
That tower strong,
And climb, and see beyond the bare
Dark branches' dearth
Spring, shaking out her golden hair,
Smile up the earth.

BAB-LOCK-HYTHE

In the time of wild roses
As up Thames we travelled
Where 'mid water-weeds ravelled
The lily uncloses,

To his old shores the river
A new song was singing,
And young shoots were springing
On old roots for ever.

Dog-daisies were dancing,
And flags flamed in cluster,
On the dark stream a lustre

Now blurred and now glancing.

A tall reed down-weighing,
The sedge-warbler fluttered;
One sweet note he uttered,
Then left it soft-swaying.

By the bank's sandy hollow
My dipt oars went beating,
And past our bows fleeting
Blue-backed shone the swallow.

High woods, heron-haunted,
Rose, changed, as we rounded
Old hills greenly mounded,
To meadows enchanted.

A dream ever moulded
Afresh for our wonder,
Still opening asunder
For the stream many-folded;

Till sunset was rimming
The West with pale flushes;
Behind the black rushes
The last light was dimming;

And the lonely stream, hiding
Shy birds, grew more lonely,
And with us was only
The noise of our gliding.

In cloud of gray weather
The evening o'erdarkened,
In the stillness we hearkened;
Our hearts sang together.

A PICTURE SEEN IN A DREAM

I saw the Goddess of the Evening pause
Between two mountain pillars. Tall as they
Appeared her stature, and her outstretched hands
Laid on those luminous cold summits, hung
Touching, and lingered. Earth was at her feet.
Her head inclined: then the slow weight of hair,
In distant hue like a waved pine-forest

Upon a mountain, down one shoulder fell.
She gazed, and there were stars within her eyes;
Not like those lights in heaven which know not what
They shine upon; but like far human hopes,
That rise beyond the end of thwarting day
In deep hearts, wronged with waste and toil, they rose;
And while beneath her from the darkening world
A vapour and a murmur silently
Floated, there came into those gazing eyes,
What should have been, were she a mortal, tears.

"BETWEEN THE MOUNTAINS AND THE PLAIN"

Between the mountains and the plain
We leaned upon a rampart old;
Beneath, branch-blossoms trembled white;
Far-off, a dusky fringe of rain
Brushed low along a sky of gold,
Where earth spread lost in endless light.

The mountains in their glory rose,
Peak thronging peak; cloud shadows mapped
The purpling brown with milky blue;
Removed, austere, shone rarer snows
Above dark ridges vapour-wrapped, —
Afar shone, Love, for me and you.

Sky-seeking mountains, boundless plain!
Old walls, and April-blossomed trees!
Of ever-young, world-ancient power,
The height, the space, was your refrain.
In us, us too, eternities
Made of that moment a white flower.

RICORDI

Of a tower, of a tower, white
In the warm Italian night,
Of a tower that shines and springs
I dream, and of our delight

Of doves, of a hundred wings
Sweeping in sound that sings
Past our faces, and wide

Returning in tremulous rings:

Of a window on Arno side,
Sun-warm when the rain has dried
On the roofs, and from far below
The clear street-cries are cried:

Of a certain court we know,
And love's and sorrow's throe
In marbles of mighty limb,
And the beat of our hearts aglow:

Of water whispering dim
To a porphyry basin's rim;
Of flowers on a windy wall
Richly tossing, I dream.

And of white towns nestling small
Upon Apennine, with a tall
Tower in the sunset air
Sounding soft vesper-call:

And of golden morning bare
On Lucca roofs, and fair
Blue hills, and scent that shook
From blossoming chestnuts, where

Red ramparts overlook
Hot meadow and leafy nook,
Where girls with laughing cries
Beat clothes in a glittering brook:

And of magic-builded skies
Upon still lagoons; and wise
Padua's pillared street
In the charm of a day that dies:

Of olive-shade in the heat,
And a lone, cool, rocky seat
On an island beach, and bright
Fresh ripples about our feet:

Of mountains in vast moon-light,
Of rivers' rushing flight,
Of gardens of green retreat
I dream, and of our delight

VENICE

White clouds that rose clouds chase
Till the sky laughs round, blue and bare;
Sunbeams that quivering waves out-race
To sparkle kisses on a marble stair;
Indolent water that images
Slender-pillared palaces,
Or glides in shadow and sun, where over
Walls that leaning crumble red
Milky blossom and fresh leaf hover,
Or glitters in endless morning spread,
Far and faint for dazzling miles
To lonely towers and cypress isles,
Where phantom mountains hang on high
Along the mist of northern sky:
O Love, what idle tale is told
That these are glories famed and old?
For to-day I know it is all in you,
This vision bathed in magic blue,
My sea that girdles me round and round
With winding arms in deeps profound,
And bears our thoughts like golden sails
To be lost where the far verge gleams and pales,
My sky that over the mountains brings
The stars, and gives us wondrous wings,
My dawn that pierces the secret night
To the central heart of burning light
And thousand-coloured flames and flowers
In radiant palaces, domes, and towers!
A marvel born of sky and sea,
Tis all in you, that have given it me.

DAWN BY THE SEA

Beautiful, cold, freshness of light reveals
The black masts, mirrored with their shadowy spars,
The hill-gloom and the sleeping wharf, and steals
Up magical faint heights of fading stars.

I hear the waves, on the long shingle thrown,
Slowly draw backward, plunge, and never cease.
Against that sea-sound the earth-stillness lone
Builds vaster in the early light's increase.

O falling blind waves, in my heart you break;
Outcast and far from my own self I seem,
With alien sense in a strange air awake,
The body and projection of a dream.

Turn back, pale Dawn, or bring that light to me
Which yesterday was lost beyond the sea.

WANDERERS

O there are wanderers over wave and strand
Invisible and secret, everywhere
Moving through light and night from land to land,
Swifter than bird or cloud upon the air.

Wild Longings from divided bosoms rent
Rush home, and Sighs crushed from the pain of years.
Far o'er their quarry hover Hates intent;
Wing to and fro world-wandering great Fears,

Pities like dew, Thoughts on their lonely road
Glide, and dark forms of spiritual Desire,
Yea, all that from its house of flesh the goad
Of terrible Love drives out in mist and fire.

Ah, souls of men and women, where is home,
That in a want, a prayer, a cry, you roam?

THE CRUSADER

Effigy mailed and mighty beneath thy mail
That liest asleep with hand upon carved sword-hilt
As ready to waken and strong to stand and hail
Death, where hosts are shaken and hot life spilt;
Here in the pillared peace thy fathers built
On English ground, amid guardian trees, though rent
This eve with gusts that yellowing boughs dishevel
And over this chantry roof make shuddering revel —
With lips of stone thou smilest; art thou content?

Still burns thy soul for battle as then, when first,
Tost upon shipboard, far thine eyes descried
The hills of the land of longing? Still dost thirst
To leap on the Paynim armies and break their pri de

For God smote in thee, God was upon thy side?
Still flame the spears through dust and blood and roar?
Still ridest slaying, filled with holy rages,
Glorying even now to hear through Time's lost ages
Thy deeds yet thundering like sea-surf on shore?

Or dost thou rather, a soul made great and mild,
Behold it all as a clashing of swords by night
Warring to save but an empty grave exiled, —
Not there, not thus, to reach the abiding Light
The City of God shines always fair and white,
By alien hosts impossible to be won;
For how should the pure be pure if these could soil it,
Or the holy holy, and ravage of this world spoil it?
A thousand storms pass from us, but not the sun.

Thou smilest mute: but I in the gloom that hearken
To loud wild gusts that, rioting blindly, tear
Soft leaves and scatter them over fields that darken,
I feel in my heart the wound of Earth's despair.
So torn from youth is trampled the innocent prayer;
So loveliest things find soonest enemies; so
Desire that kindled the shaping mind to fashion
Our hope afresh, pours infinite out its passion,
And the world it has striven for breaks it with blow on blow.

The fool, in his multitude mighty, exults to maim
Greatness; heroes under the world's slow wheel
Fall; the timorous how they seek to tame
Tongues that fear not, hearts that burn and feel!
Slaves conspire to enslave; and, last appeal,
The deaf have power, the blind authority; yea,
They blind the seer, lest they too see his vision,
And all their works be turned to a God's derision;
Beholding this, who would cry not, Up and slay!

O yet my faith is fixt, that the best is chosen,
And truth by joy is kissed as certain good,
And love, even love, though a million hearts be frozen,
Love, weak, and shamed, and tortured, is understood.
Yea, powers are with us when we are most withstood.
Not vainly the soul in beauty and hope confides;
And if it were not so, then had thought no haven,
Nor the brave heart wisdom nor warrant above the craven:
Mid all these woes the City of God abides.

But O to win there, far how far it seems!
And often, as thou, O pilgrim knight, I long

For a land remote, and to be where perfect dreams
Of the soul are acts as natural as a song
In a singer's mouth, and joy need fear no wrong.
And, tossing upon my restless thoughts, I vow
My heart away from a world that would undo me.
Then lo, in a hush some voice divine thrills through me,
"O heart of little faith, seek here, seek now!"

Yes, here and now! But how to attain, when fierce
In power and pain Time and the World oppose?
With what shall the soul be weaponed, her way to pierce
To her one desire through many embattled foes?
Must all in a waste of strife and of hatred close?
Shall love unfriended hide, and longing droop,
And all our strength be poured in a conflict sterile,
For the world's hard conquest youth's dear hope imperil,
And the soul to an alien use ignobly stoop?

Thou knowest, Crusader; O thy smile knows all.
Love takes no sword to battle, for Love is flame,
Itself a sword, upon whose edge falsehoods fall;
A peace that troubles, a joy that puts to shame.
Though the soul be at war for ever, she burns to an aim,
The world has none! We are wronged, but endure; we bleed,
But conquer; hatred is idle as vain compliance:
We know not Time, who have made the great affiance.
To die for that we live for is life indeed.

SOLITUDE

The stag that lifted up his kingly head
Upon the silent mountains, and from far
Beneath him heard the confident harsh cry
Of men invading his old solitudes,
Then bounding over the rough slopes has climbed
By dancing brooks remoter ranges, thick
With forests moaning in the cloudy winds
Of desolate November, nor has stayed
Till on the utmost craggy ledge, among
Wet boughs, with antlers dripping from the mist
And with sweat-darkened quivering coat he snuffs
Wide-nostrilled the wild air, where motionless
He stands at last; what shudder as of joy
Deeply to breathe that native loneliness
Possesses him! From reddened oaks around
Lost leaves are torn innumerably and whirled,

Fast as from hearts of men their fearful hopes,
Into the drizzling gulf; he hears beyond
From cliffs that dimly tower in abrupt
Strange precipices, the world-ancient roar
Of headlong torrents: now the vapour rolls
Blank over all, now rending it a gust
Reveals by golden glimpses the pale stream
Poured in a trembling pillar, at whose foot
The snowy seethe shoots forward and recoils
For one tumultuous moment, then again
Arches into one pure unfretted wave
And sends a voice in splendour down the gorge.

"BLUE MOON SHINES O'ER THE SEA"

Blue noon shines o'er the sea;
Waves break starry on the sand;
Lights and sounds and scents come free
On the radiant air of the land.
I am filled with the melody of waves
That take my heart onward in tune;
My heart follows yearning after, and craves
No other delight nor boon.

They enfold the earth in desire
With a closer and closer kiss;
From life into life they expire,
In dying their birth and their bliss.
I am melted in them, I am filled
f With the passion in peace they have found.
Even so would my spirit in peace be thrilled
So be lost in a love without bound.

Peace is no tame dove
To be caught and caged in the breast,
No, nor untamable Love
In a moment lightly possest
Peace is wide and wild,
And Love without master as the sea;
He is soft in his ways as a little child,
Yet is mightier far than we.

"O MY PEACE"

O my peace, O well
So deep no thought could sound it,
Whence arose thy spell
When in my heart I found it?

Like a coral isle
That long silent grew
From deepest deeps, the while
Slept or stormed the blue,

Emerging to enfold
Peace answering the skies,
And ringed with rock, where rolled
All day the white surge cries,

Till from isles unknown
Far on spicy air
Seeds in secret blown
Sprang to beauty there.

O my love, my sky,
That with soft breath broughtest
Bloom that cannot die,
Of my life thou wroughtest

Such an isle that rings
A peace within so dear,
Howe'er the strong world flings,
Without, his surges drear,

To my heart, whose core
Thy love in joy entrances,
Like music the world's baffled roar
Only this peace enhances. .

FLOWER AND VOICE

Tremulous out of that long darkness, how
Wast thou, O blossom, made
Upon the wintry bough?
What drew thee to appear,
Like a thought in the mind,
Ignorant, unafraid,
And perfect? — Yet the wind
Blew on thee how sharp! how drear
The drops fell from the sudden-clouded spring!

Those delicate rare petals, all storm-thrilled,
Shone into recollection, when my ear
From a half-opened door was filled
With a voice singing; floating up to sing
A song, long ago from a heart's darkness born
And upon young lips born again;
A voice, flowering clear
In beauty stolen from the world of pain.

Ah, not to-night of beauty I thought,
Yet beautiful beyond all hope's desire,
O wonderful, more wonderful to me
Than any miracle of beauty wrought
Was my Love's voice, saying beside the fire,
Where she leaned by my knee,
Dear, broken words; words of no art,
And yet in them was all my want, I found;
Life has no more to give than that sweet sound
Breaking and melting deep in my heart's heart

THE DARK GARDEN

When your head leans back slowly, and gazing eyes
Muse earnest upon mine and starry swim
With depths unfathomed that still well and rise,
And the words fail, and sight with love grows dim,

Whence comes that almost sadness, almost wound
Of joy, whose thoughts sink like the wearied flight
Of birds on seas, lost in love's deeps profound,
Inscrutable as odours blown through night?

We know not: and we know not whence love rose,
Pouring its beauty over us, as the moon
On this dim garden rises, and none knows
Where she was wandering, those blind nights of June.

Hush, hush, the mystery of life is here!
Oursacred joy kisses our sacred fear.

PARTING AND MEETING

When we are parted, the world ails.

Life wants, the pulse of it falls slack;
The wind stings, and the clouds roll black;
Wishes fly far as absent sails;
And in the mind old mournful tales
Murmur, and toss an echo back.
In all things fair is found some lack.
Light cares grow heavy, and pleasure stales.

But when from far in the thronged street
Our eyes each other leap to find,
O when at last our arms enwind,
And on our lips our longings meet,
The world glows new with each heart-beat,
Love is come home, Life is enshrined.

Deep in these thoughts, more tender than a sky
Whose light ebbs far as in futurity,
Deep, deeper yet my blessed spirit steep,
Singing of you still; you and only you
Gave me to breathe and touch and taste, all true,
Love from the utmost height and deepest deep
In my own heart, as all that summer knows
Of glory and perfume hides in one shut rose.

You and you only gave me, Dearest, this.
A pressure of the hand, a silent kiss,
And all is well; the hurt, the pain-pricks healed;
And rapt and hushed, as from some green recess
Into a golden solitariness,
All ours, we look; and suddenly revealed
Is all that we in our desire might be,
Winged and immortal, fretting to be free.

Then in that large, appeasing air we grow
Near to Love's greatness, and our hearts outflow.
We are as those who traffic with the sea;
Washed from our liberated spirits is all
That the feared world made stagnant, pent or small,
For love has touched us with his majesty:
We grow beyond the bounds of time and pain,
Then in one heart-beat wondering meet again.

DAY'S END

When I am weary, thronged with the cares of the vain day
That tease as harsh winds tease the unresting autumn boughs,

I still my mind at evening and put all else away
But the image of my Love, where all my hopes I house.

The thoughts of her fall gently as the gentleness of snow
That after storm makes smoothness in the ways that are rough;
White with a hush of beauty over my heart they grow
To the peace of which my heart can never hold enough.

"IN MISTY BLUE THE DARK IS HEARD"

In misty blue the lark is heard
Above the silent homes of men;
The bright-eyed thrush, the little wren,
The yellow-billed sweet-voiced blackbird
Mid sallow blossoms blond as curd
Or silver oak boughs, carolling
With happy throat from tree to tree,
Sing into light this morn of spring
That sang my dear love home to me.

Be starry, buds of clustered white,
Around the dark waves of her hair!
The young fresh glory you prepare
Is like my ever-fresh delight
When she comes shining on my sight
With meeting eyes, with such a cheek
As colours fair like flushing tips
Of shoots, and music ere she speak
Lies in the wonder of her lips.

Airs of the morning, breathe about
Keen faint scents of the wild wood side
From thickets where primroses hide
Mid the brown leaves of winters rout.
Chestnut and willow, beacon out
For joy of her, from far and nigh,
Your English green on English hills:
Above her head, song-quivering sky,
And at her feet, the daffodils.

Because she breathed, the world was more,
And breath a finer soul to use,
And life held lovelier hopes to choose:
But O to-day my heart brims o'er,
Earth glows as from a kindled core,
Like shadows of diviner things

Are hill and cloud and flower and tree —
A splendour that is hers and spring's, —
The day my love came home to me.

Hide me in your heart, Love,
None but we can know
How with every heart-beat
Love could grow and grow

Till the seed that branched abroad,
How, we could not guess,
Holds us in the shadow
Of its boughs that bless;

And the stars and mountains,
Earth and chanting sea
Seem a mighty music
Sung to you and me;

Time-forgotten meaning,
Poured for us apart,
Murmured out of all the world
To our secret heart

Hide within my heart, Love.
Never may I know

My heart's beat from your heart's beat,
No, nor throe from throe!

THE CRUCIBLE

Because thou earnest, Love, to break
The strong mould of this world in two,
And of the senseless fragments take
And in thy mighty music make
A world more wondrous and more true,
Now my soul hath taken wings,
Newly bathed in light intense,
And purging off the film of sense,
Of its native glory sings.
And that inward vision, turning

Pomps of earth to vapour brief,
Sees as in a furnace burning
Time, a swiftly shrivelled leaf:
Sees the fortressed city fall
To a mound of nameless wall,
Shrining temple, columned porch
Life-bought gems, and royal gold,
Shake like ashes from a torch;
Palaces, world-envied thrones,
Crumble down to dust as old
And idle as Behemoth's bones
On a frozen mountain-top.

I see the very mountains drop,
Wasting with their weight of stones
Swifter than a torrent slides,
Melted like the crimson cloud
Vanishing about their sides
When the morn has burst his shroud.

Love, Love, because thou didst destroy
So much, and madest so much vain,
I know what lives and shall remain,
I see amid Time's gorgeous wane
The dawn and promise of my joy.
lift me thither, lift me higher!
I am not save in this desire,
Lost and living, fire in fire.

"I WANT A THOUSAND THINGS"

I want a thousand things to-night;
The bonds of earth are strict and strong;
Yet glory were a vain delight
Did you not sing within my song.

Hungers, despairs, and victories,
All the world's glories and alarms,
Forget their wound and find their prize
But on your lips, but in your arms.

A PRAYER

O Thou who seekest me

Through the day's heartless hurry and uproar,
Who followest me to my thought's farthest shore —
Nay, who art gone before —
Sustain me, O sustain
The heart that seeks for thee.
The world is filled with rendings and with pain,
But thou with peace; with peace, though wronged so sore
By our despair, blind wrath and blind disdain.
And thou hast made it dear
To hope against the wrongs of every hour,
And given to hope the power
And passion to prevail;
The heart, for all its fear,
Putting forth delicate shy flower on flower
Against the hard world's hail.
O might my love, that in one heart has found
Such hope to cherish, and such joy to sound,
O might it grow through days that chafe and bound
And our true souls from one another screen,
Till in its clear profound
Part of thy peace were seen.

MILTON

AN ODE

Soul of England, dost thou sleep,
Lulled or dulled, thy mighty youth forgotten?
Of the world's wine hast thou drunk too deep?
Hast thou sown more than thy hands can reap?
Turn again thine ear
To that song severe
In thine hour of storm and war begotten!

Here in towered London's throng,
In her streets, with Time's new murmur seething,
Milton pacing mused his haughty song.
Here he sleeps out feud and fret and wrong.
Nay, that spirit august
Tramples death's low dust,
Still for us is kindled, burning, breathing.

He, on whose earth-darkened sight
Rose horizons of the empyrean
And the ordered spheres' unhasting flight;
He, who saw where, round the heart of Light

Seraphs ardent-eyed
Flamed in circle wide,
Quiring music of their solemn paean,

When through space a trouble ran
(Like a flush on serene skies arisen)
That from this dim spot of earth began—
Rumour of the world's new marvel, Man,
From whose heart's beat sped
Hope, hazard, and dread
Past earth's borders to hell's fiery prison:

He, who saw the Anarch's hate
Tower, winged for woe; the serpent charming
Eve in her imperilled bower; the Gate
Barred, and those two forms that, desolate
Mid the radiant spheres,
Wept first human tears;
Earlier war in heaven, and angels arming:

He who, like his Samson, bowed,
Toiling, hardly-tasked and night-enfolded,
Steered his proud course to one purpose vowed,
As an eagle beats through hailing cloud
Strong-winged and alone,
Seeking skies unknown:
He whose verse, majestically moulded,

Moves like armed and bannered host
Streaming irresistible, or abounding
River in a land's remoteness lost,
Poured from solitary peaks of frost,
And far histories brings
Of old realms and kings,
With high fates of fallen Man resounding:

This is England's voice that rang
Over Europe; this the soul unshaken
That from darkness a great splendour sang,
Beauty mightier for the cost and pang;
Of our blood and name
Risen, our spirits to claim,
To enlarge, to summon, to awaken!

THE BATTLE OF STAMFORD BRIDGE

"Haste thee, Harold, haste thee North!
Norway ships in Humber crowd.
Tall Hardrada, Sigurd's son,
For thy ruin this hath done —
England for his own hath vowed.

"The earls have fought, the earls are fled.
From Tyne to Ouse the homesteads flame.
York behind her battered wall
Waits the instant of her fall
And the shame of England's name.

"Traitor Tosti's banner streams
With the invading Raven's wing;
Black the land and red the skies
Where Northumbria bleeds and cries
For thy vengeance, England's King!"

Since that frighted summons flew
Not twelve suns have sprung and set
Northward marching night and day
Has King Harold kept his way.
The hour is come; the hosts are met

Morn through thin September mist
Flames on moving helm and man.
On either side of Derwenfs banks
Are the Northmen's shielded ranks.
But silent stays the English van.

A rider to Earl Tosti comes:
"Turn thee, Tosti, to thy kin!
Harold thy brother brings thee sign
All Northumbria shall be thine.
Make thy peace, ere the fray begin!"

"And if I turn me to my kin
And if I stay the Northmen's hand,
What will Harold give to my friend this day?
To Norway's king what price will he pay
Out of this English land?"

That rider laughed a mighty laugh.
"Six full feet of English soil!
Or, since he is taller than the most,
Seven feet shall he have to boast;
This Harold gives for Norway's spoil."

"What rider was he that spoke thee fair?"
Harold Hardrada to Tosti cried.
"It was Harold of England spoke me fair;
But now of his bane let him beware.
Set on, set on! we will break his pride."

Sudden arrows flashed and flew;
Dark lines of English leapt and rushed
With sound of storm that stung like hail,
And steel rang sharp on supple mail
With thrust that pierced and blow that crushed.

And sullenly back in a fierce amaze
The Northmen gave to the river side.
The main of their host on the further shore
Could help them nothing, pressed so sore.
In the ooze they fought, in the wave they died.

On a narrow bridge alone one man
The English mass and fury stays.
The spears press close, the timber cracks,
But high he swings his dreadful axe,
With every stroke a life he slays;

Till pierced at last from the stream below
He falls: the Northmen break and shout.
Forward they hurl in wild onset.
But as struggling fish in a mighty net
The English hem them round about.

Now Norway's king grew battle-mad,
Mad with joy of his strength he smote.
But as he hewed his battle-path,
And heaped the dead men for a swath,
An arrow clove him through the throat;

And where he slaughtered, red he fell.
O then was Norway's hope undone,
Doomed men were they that fought in vain,
Hardrada slain, and Tosti slain!
The field was lost, the field was won.

York this night rings all her bells,
Harold feasts within her halls.
The Captains lift their wine-cups. — Hark!
What hoofs come thudding through the dark
And sudden stop? What silence falls?

Spent with riding staggers in
One who cries: "Fell news I bring.
Duke William has o'erpast the sea.
His host is camped at Pevensey.
Save us, save England now, O King!"

Woe to Harold! Twice 'tis not
His to conquer and to save.
Well he knows the lot is cast.
England claims him to the last.
South he marches to his grave.

GLORIOUS HEART

Swift and straight as homing dove,
Heedless, so its flight be flown,
All the full stream of thy love,
Love that knows no mortal bounding,
Pours, is emptied for its own,
Glorious Heart,
Great and loyal and abounding!

Over stormy waters eager
Lifted like a breasting prow,
Though the winds and waves beleaguer,
To one star thy true course guiding
Onward, ever onward, thou
Glorious Heart,
Steerest, hopest, well confiding.

When thy strength within thee faints,
When to grief the way is hard,
All thy heroes and thy saints,
Lo, with strong hands arming for thee,
Hold thy tenderness in guard,
Glorious Heart!
They that bore thy pains before thee.

Like a flag that, battle-girt,
Keeps its ardent colours high,
Knows not either hate or hurt,
Nay, nor fear nor thought of turning,
Flag for which men leap to die,
Glorious Heart,
Still within my heart be burning!

Robert Laurence Binyon, CH, was born on August 10th, 1869 in Lancaster in Lancashire, England to Quaker parents, Frederick Binyon and Mary Dockray.

He studied at St Paul's School, London before enrolling at Trinity College, Oxford, to read classics.

Binyon's first published work was Persephone in 1890. Whilst only a few pages in length it certainly illustrated the talents that Binyon would develop as a poet even though he continued to advance multiple career opportunities.

Immediately after graduating in 1893, Binyon started work at the British Museum for the Department of Printed Books, writing catalogues for the museum and art monographs for himself. As well as being one of England's best poets he was also renowned for his knowledge of various arts particularly with regard to Japan and Persia.

His first poetry book Lyric Poems was published in 1894.

In 1895 his first art book, Dutch Etchers of the Seventeenth Century, was published and, that same year, Binyon moved into the Museum's Department of Prints and Drawings.

Whilst Binyon became known to a wide audience as a poet his output was not prodigious. In 1898, Porphyrion & Other Poems was published followed by Odes (1901) and The Death of Adam & Other Poems (1904).

That same year, 1904, Binyon married the historian Cicely Margaret Powell. The union was to produce three daughters.

In the early years of the 20th Century Binyon was a regular patron of the Wiener Cafe of London together with fellow artists and intellectuals; Ezra Pound, Sir William Rothenstein, Walter Sickert, Charles Ricketts, Lucien Pissarro and Edmund Dulac.

His poetic work continued despite the demands of the British Museum and his other interests. London Visions was published in 1908 followed by England & Other Poems in 1909.

His work at the British Museum ensured promotions were a frequent occurrence for Binyon. In 1909, he became its Assistant Keeper, and in 1913 he was made the Keeper of the new Sub-Department of Oriental Prints and Drawings.

It was also at this time that he played a crucial role in the formation of Modernism in London by introducing young Imagist poets such as Ezra Pound, Richard Aldington and H.D. (Hilda Doolittle) to East Asian visual art and literature.

Many of Binyon's books produced while at the Museum were influenced by his own sensibilities as a poet, although some are clearly works of plain scholarship, such as his four volume catalogue of all the Museum's English drawings, and his seminal catalogue of Chinese and Japanese prints.

Binyon's poetic reputation before the war, although built on several slim volumes, was such that, on the death of the Poet Laureate Alfred Austin in 1913, Binyon was among the names considered as his likely successor. It was quite a field. Among the other illustrious contenders were Thomas Hardy, John Masefield and Rudyard Kipling; however the post was awarded to Robert Bridges.

Moved and shaken by the onset of the World War I and its military tactics of young men slaughtered to hold or gain a few yards of shell-shocked mud as the British Expeditionary Force began its campaign Binyon wrote his seminal poem For the Fallen, with its Ode of Remembrance (the third and fourth or simply the fourth stanza of the poem). The poem was published by The Times newspaper on September 21st, when public feeling was shaken by the recent Battle of Marne. It became an instant classic, turning moments of great loss into a National and human tribute.

Today, For the Fallen, is often recited at Remembrance Sunday services as well as being an integral part of Anzac Day services in Australia and New Zealand and of November 11th Remembrance Day services in Canada. The "Ode of Remembrance" is now acknowledged as a tribute to all casualties of war, irrespective of nation.

In 1915, despite being too old to enlist, Binyon volunteered at a British hospital for French soldiers, the Hôpital Temporaire d'Arc-en-Barrois, Haute-Marne, France, working for a short time as a hospital orderly.

He returned there in the summer of 1916 and took care of soldiers taken in from the Verdun battlefield. He wrote about his experiences in For Dauntless France (1918) and his poems, "Fetching the Wounded" and "The Distant Guns", were inspired by his hospital service.

After the war, he returned to the British Museum and wrote numerous books on art; especially on William Blake, Persian and Japanese art. His work on ancient Japanese and Chinese cultures offered inspiration that inspired many, among them the poets Ezra Pound and W. B. Yeats. His work on Blake and his followers kept alive the then nearly-forgotten memory of the work of Samuel Palmer. Binyon's spectrum of interests continued the traditional interest of British visionary Romanticism in the rich strangeness of Mediterranean and Oriental cultures.

In 1931, his two volume Collected Poems appeared and by 1932, Binyon was promoted to the post of Keeper of the Prints and Drawings Department. The following year, 1933, he retired from the British Museum. He went to live in the country at Westridge Green, near Streatley but continued writing poetry.

In 1933–1934, Binyon was appointed Norton Professor of Poetry at Harvard University. He delivered a series of lectures on The Spirit of Man in Asian Art, which were published in 1935.

Binyon continued his academic work: in May, 1939 he gave the prestigious Romanes Lecture in Oxford on Art and Freedom, and in 1940 he was appointed the Byron Professor of English Literature at the University of Athens. He worked there until forced to leave by the German invasion of Greece in April, 1941.

Binyon had been friends with Ezra Pound for a long time, and in the 1930s the two became especially close; Pound affectionately called him "BinBin", and he assisted Binyon with his translation of Dante.

Between 1933 and 1943, Binyon published his acclaimed translation of Dante's Divine Comedy in an English version of terza rima, made with some editorial assistance by Ezra Pound. It was acknowledged for many decades as *the* popular translation for Dante readers.

During the horrors of the Second World War Binyon wrote a poem that many claim as to be a masterpiece 'The Burning of the Leaves', puts in print his lines on the London Blitz.

At his death Binyon was working on a major three-part Arthurian trilogy, the first part of which was published after his death as The Madness of Merlin (1947).

Robert Laurence Binyon died in Dunedin Nursing Home, Bath Road, Reading, on March 10th, 1943 after undergoing an operation. A funeral service was held at Trinity College Chapel, Oxford, on March 13th, 1943.

Binyon's ashes were scattered at St. Mary's Church, Aldworth.

On November 11th, 1985, Binyon was among sixteen poets of the Great War commemorated on a slate stone unveiled in Westminster Abbey's Poets' Corner. The inscription on the stone quotes a fellow Great War poet, Wilfred Owen. It reads: "My subject is War, and the pity of War. The Poetry is in the pity."

Laurence Binyon – A Concise Bibliography

Poems and Verse
Persephone (1890)
Lyric Poems (1894)
The Praise of Life (1896)
Porphyrion & Other Poems (1898)
Odes (1901)
Death of Adam & Other Poems (1904)
Penthesilea (1905)
London Visions (1908)
England & Other Poems (1909)
Auguries (1913)
For The Fallen (The Times, September 21st, 1914)
The Winnowing Fan (1914)
The Anvil (1916)
The Cause (1917)
The New World: Poems (1918)
The Secret: Sixty Poems (1920)
The Idols (1928)
Collected Poems Vol I: London Visions, Narrative Poems, Translations (1931)
Collected Poems Vol II: Lyrical Poems (1931)
The North Star & Other Poems (1941)
The Burning of the Leaves & Other Poems (1944)
The Madness of Merlin (1947)

Poems Set to Music

In 1915 Cyril Rootham set "For the Fallen" for chorus and orchestra, first performed in 1919 by the Cambridge University Musical Society conducted by the composer.

Edward Elgar set to music "The Fourth of August", "To Women", and "For the Fallen", as The Spirit of England, Op. 80, for tenor or soprano solo, chorus and orchestra (1917).

English Arts and Myth

Dutch Etchers of the Seventeenth Century (1895), Binyon's first book on painting
John Crone and John Sell Cotman (1897)
William Blake: Being all his Woodcuts Photographically Reproduced in Facsimile (1902)
English Poetry in its relation to painting and the other arts (1918)
Drawings and Engravings of William Blake (1922)
Arthur: A Tragedy (1923)
The Followers of William Blake (1925)
The Engraved Designs of William Blake (1926)
Landscape in English Art and Poetry (1931)
English Watercolours (1933)
Gerard Hopkins and his influence (1939)
Art and freedom. (The Romanes lecture, delivered 25 May 1939). Oxford: The Clarendon press, (1939)

Japanese and Persian Arts

Painting in the Far East (1908)
Japanese Art (1909)
Flight of the Dragon (1911)
The Court Painters of the Grand Moguls (1921)
Japanese Colour Prints (1923)
The Poems of Nizami (1928) (Translation)
Persian Miniature Painting (1933)
The Spirit of Man in Asian Art (1936)
Autobiography[edit]
For Dauntless France (1918) (War memoir)

Biography

Botticelli (1913)
Akbar (1932)

Stage Plays

Brief Candles A verse-drama about the decision of Richard III to dispatch his two nephews
Paris and Œnone. A Tragedy in One Act (1906)
Godstow Nunnery: Play
Boadicea; A Play in eight Scenes

Attila: A Tragedy in Four Acts (1907)
Ayuli: A Play in three Acts and an Epilogue
Sophro the Wise: A Play for Children
(Most of the above were written for John Masefield's theatre).

www.ingramcontent.com/pod-product-compliance
Lightning Source LLC
Chambersburg PA
CBHW060056050426
42448CB00011B/2489